Japanese

✦ FOLK MAGIC ✦

Publisher
Balthazar Pagani

Graphic design and layout
Bebung

Editing and fact checking Giulia Bilancetti

Vivida

Vivida® is a registered trademark property of White Star s.r.l.

© 2026 White Star s.r.l.
Piazzale Luigi Cadorna, 6
20123 Milano, Italy
www.whitestar.it

Translation: Contextus S.r.l., Pavia (Daniela Innocenti)
Editing: Abby Young

ISBN 978-88-544-2183-7
1 2 3 4 5 6   30 29 28 27 26

Printed in China

Marianna Zanetta
and Asuka Ozumi

Japanese

✦ FOLK MAGIC ✦

ILLUSTRATIONS BY
Danilo Kato

Vivida

Table of Contents

(✦)

Folk Magic in Japan

(+)

Japan is a land of diverse and captivating religious and spiritual traditions, distinct from those of the West. Over the centuries, it has been a place where various schools of thought and ascetic practices have coexisted and intertwined through syncretism. The archipelago's two religions are Shintō and Buddhism.

Shintō, often regarded as Japan's indigenous faith, is a form of animism centered on *kami* – spiritual beings or deities that inhabit natural places, objects, and phenomena. Buddhism, on the other hand, originated in India and reached Japan via Korea, which, over the centuries, introduced esoteric practices influenced by Chinese traditions.

Alongside these religions, there are traditions where boundaries dissolve and distinctions become fluid.

This realm of folk and shamanic practices is inhabited by marginal figures and steeped in wonder — a space where ascetics and *miko* venture into the vast and sometimes perilous spirit world. Here, ghosts, *bakemono*, and *yōkai* coexist with *kami* and Buddhas, who at times enter the human realm — beings from whom, on occasion, we may even need protection.

Japanese folk magic is deeply embedded in this multifaceted religious and spiritual landscape.

However, when we speak of magic in Japan, it is important to recognize that its traditions differ significantly from those in the West. This distinction is reflected in the terminology itself: *mahō*, *majutsu*, *jūjutsu*, *noroi*, and *yōjutsu* are just some of the words that describe a complex and nuanced world of magical arts.

The multiplicity of terms and practices corresponds to a host of figures.

In this land we meet many characters, both male and female, who over the centuries have established themselves as experts in these rites, in a way becoming guardians of the threshold between the human and spiritual worlds. *Miko, minkan fusha, shugenja, onmyōji*: with their in-depth knowledge of magical arts, they all shift between institutions and folk practices.

Alongside them, we find various historical and legendary figures endowed with great magical powers, such as Himiko and Shōtoku Taishi, as well as numerous deities like Amaterasu and Ame no Uzume. And of course, we cannot overlook the rich world of *yōkai* — supernatural creatures, both fearsome and mysterious, that sometimes aid humans in securing their well-being or, at times, indulge their thirst for vengeance. From *kitsune* to *tengu*, these spirits can be benevolent, but they are just as often mischievous or even dangerous, shaping the way humans interact with nature and the world around them.

The allure of these practices lives on in Japan.

Particularly since the postwar period, the country has rediscovered various magical and esoteric traditions while also embracing diverse influences from the West — we need only think of the fascination with tarot cards.

This powerful and syncretic dimension remains alive, reflecting — through rituals, beliefs, and symbols — the deep connection between humans and the supernatural, between the visible and the invisible, in an ongoing process of rediscovery and creation.

(✦)

MAGIC

(✦)

In Japan, the supernatural is shaped by a rich tapestry of traditions and influences. Thanks to its diverse religious heritage and several loans from neighboring cultures, this world merges Shintō and Buddhist beliefs with Taoist and Chinese-derived practices. Throughout Japan's centuries-old history, a wide range of supernatural figures have existed both within institutional structures and on society's fringes. On one hand, the age-old practice of *onmyōdō* (the way of Yin and Yang) and Esoteric Buddhism (known as *mikkyō*) were deeply intertwined with court life and imperial traditions. On the other hand, *shugendō* (the ascetic, mountain-dwelling lifestyle) and a vast repertoire of folk beliefs — such as the Night of Kōshin — offer a glimpse into a more fluid, syncretic world shaped by continuous cultural influences. This captivating universe still seems to guard the secret soul of Japan.

(✦)

Onmyōdō

*O*nmyōdō, the way of Yin and Yang, is a tradition of Chinese origins bringing together natural sciences, occult practices, and Taoist philosophies. It was introduced to Japan in the sixth century and was initially seen as a divination technique. Over time, it incorporated local Shintō and Buddhist elements. At its core, *onmyōdō* revolves around the duality of two complementary yet opposing forces (Yin and Yang) and the five elements (wood, water, fire, metal, earth) used to maintain harmony and balance.

The practitioners, known as *onmyōdō*, were regarded as masters of magic and divination, skilled in reading celestial signs and influencing events. They often held prestigious court positions and were tasked with regulating the calendar, practicing divination, and protecting against evil spirits. The most famous is undoubtedly Abe no Seimei (921–1005, see p. 101); after his death, a shrine was dedicated to him in Kyōto.

Though *onmyōdō* was officially abolished in 1870, during the Meji period (1868–1912), it survived in folklore and religious traditions. Since the mid-20th century, it has gained renewed attention, particularly through its portrayal in Japanese popular culture.

(+)

The Three Imperial Regalia

The Three Imperial Regalia (Sanshu no Jingi) are the ultimate symbols of the emperor and his legitimacy as the rightful heir of the great goddess Amaterasu. Shrouded in mystery, these objects have never been seen by anyone.

Kusanagi no Tsurugi, the sword symbolizing courage and strength, was discovered by Susanō inside the body of the serpent Yamata no Orochi. Centuries later, it came into the possession of Yamato Takeru (72?–114, see p. 99), given to him by his aunt. It is from him that the sword takes its name, Kusanagi. The sword is said to be enshrined at Atsuta Shrine in Nagoya, though some accounts claim it was lost at sea in the 12th century.

Yata no Kagami, the mirror symbolizing wisdom and truth, was the artifact that lured Amaterasu out of her hiding place, restoring light to the world. Likely a Bronze Age artifact, it is believed to be kept at Ise Shrine.

Lastly, Yasakani no Magatama is the sacred jewel that was hung alongside the mirror in front of Amaterasu's hiding place. A symbol of benevolence and compassion, it is thought to be a jade necklace housed within the Imperial Palace.

(+)

The Night of Kōshin

According to Taoism, three worms live in the human body: their appearances may vary depending on the tradition, but each is believed to cause harm and ageing to both the body and the soul. During the Night of Kōshin (which occurs every 60 days), the three worms emerge from the person's sleeping body to report their actions to the Celestial Emperor, who punishes their misdeeds by shortening their lifespan.

This belief originated in China during the Heian period (794–1185), later becoming rooted in Japan during the Edō period (1603–1868), when the village inhabitants began to gather and keep watch during the Night of Kōshin (the practice known as *kōshinmachi* or *kōshinkō*). The purpose of these gatherings was to ensure that the worms did not leave the bodies.

Despite its Taoist origins, this belief incorporates Buddhist traditions and figures, such as Shōmen Kongō – one of the Five Wise Rulers – and the popular *sanzaru*, the three wise monkeys from the Buddhist saying: "See no evil, hear no evil, speak no evil."

(+)

Noroi Curses

*N*oroi refers to practices of cursing through the conjuring up of supernatural forces (such as *kami* or powerful spirits) to influence a person's fate or seek revenge on an enemy. Traces of these practices can be found as far back as the *Nihonshoki* (*Chronicles of Japan*, 720 AD) and in various archaeological finds from the eighth century.

In these practices, talismans or ritual objects were placed on a person (or a straw doll representing them) or at the location affected by the curse. These curses carried negative connotations and were highly harmful to individuals and communities. They have been considered illegal since. Indeed, the *Taihō Code* of 701 AD included prohibitions and punishments for those who engaged in such sorcery.

Over the centuries, various methods developed to break or neutralize *noroi* curses. For example, salt (a purifying element in Shintō) would be sprinkled at the entrance or gate of a home, or *onmyōji* masters would be consulted to rebalance energies.

(+)

Esoteric Buddhism

Known as Shingon, Esoteric Buddhism (*mikkyō*) was introduced to Japan from China in the ninth century by the monk Kūkai (774–835), also known by his posthumous name, Kōbō Daishi. It is a form of Buddhism that combines doctrinal teachings with meditation and physical practices, based on the belief that enlightenment can be attained during earthly life.

Shingon Buddhism makes extensive use of *mantras* (recited formulas), *mudras* (hand positions), and *mandala* (graphic representations of the universe) to aid meditation: the goal is to awaken spiritual powers, purify the mind, and attain Buddhahood. A well-known ritual is the *goma*, a fire ceremony aimed at restoring the health of the community and the nation. This and other practices later influenced other traditions, such as Zen and *shugendō*.

A central place of worship is Mount Kōya, where the Kongōji temple complex was founded in 819 and is still active today. Shingon Buddhism continues to be meaningful, and there are several places of worship associated with it, including the 88 temples on Shikoku Island — the destination of a famous pilgrimage.

(+)

Shugendō

Shugendō is a syncretic practice that combines elements of Buddhism, Taoism, and Japanese shamanic traditions. Its origins are uncertain, but it likely stems from an ancient mountain cult and the ascetics (*hijiri*) who practiced in isolation, engaging with the spirit world.

The semi-legendary figure associated with the founding of *shugendō* is En no Gyōja, who lived during the Nara period (710–794), though the tradition later solidified during the Heian period. Practitioners, called *yamabushi* or *shugenja*, would retreat to the mountains to undergo intense ascetic practices, such as pilgrimages to remote areas or isolation during the winter months; they also performed various rituals to connect with the spiritual realms.

Sacred sites are scattered across several mountainous regions, with the most famous being Mount Haguro and Mount Yoshino, which are considered symbols of purification and enlightenment. Today, *shugendō* enjoys a renewed popularity due to a growing interest in ascetic life as a counterbalance to the hectic pace of modern society.

(✦)

RITUALS AND
PREPARATIONS

(✦)

Japan's diverse religious traditions have given rise to a rich heritage of customs and rites aimed at ensuring well-being and good fortune. These ancient practices include summoning of deities or protective spirits, using herbs, reciting *mantras* (Buddhist prayers), or even carrying amulets to ward off misfortune. This deep connection between spirituality and traditional medicine — such as *kanpō*, which has Chinese origins — reflects the belief that illnesses or natural disasters are caused by evil spirits. Many of these rituals are linked to key seasonal transitions, like *setsubun*, or to imperial traditions, like *chinkon*, reinforcing how the boundaries between institutional and folk dimensions are often more fluid than they appear. Even today, many of these folk traditions remain embedded in daily life, offering a sense of protection and guidance as people navigate life's challenges, both great and small.

(+)

Kanpō Medicine

Kanpō is a traditional form of medicine that developed in Japan in the sixth century, with deep roots in Chinese medicine. The term itself, which literally means "Chinese medicine," was coined to distinguish it from Western medicine, which began spreading during the Edō period. Its wider adoption is often attributed to the Chinese monk Jianzhen (known as Ganjin in Japanese), who arrived at the imperial court in 754 after years of travel.

Kanpō aims to restore balance and harmony within the body. The remedies used are blends of herbs, minerals, and animal-derived substances, carefully prepared according to the patient's constitution and symptoms.

After experiencing a decline during the Meiji period, when it was largely overshadowed by Western medicine, *kanpō* has since been integrated into Japan's healthcare system and is now used alongside modern medical treatments. Japanese pharmacies even have entire sections dedicated to traditional pharmacology. In recent years, *kanpō* has also been gaining popularity abroad, partly due to the global spread of practices such as acupuncture.

C+)

Reiki

Reiki is an energy healing practice that emerged in Japan in the 20ᵗʰ century, based on the teachings of Mikao Usui (1865–1926). After fasting for three weeks on Mount Kurama, near Kyoto, Usui claimed to have reached a state similar to enlightenment. On his way back, he realized he had acquired a healing ability through the laying on of hands.

Shortly afterward, he founded a school to spread what he called "Reiki therapy"; the term combines *rei* (soul or spirit) and *ki* (vital energy). The core idea behind his teachings is that energy flows through the body and that any interruption of this flow can lead to physical, emotional, or spiritual discomfort.

One of Usui's disciples passed his teachings on to Hawayo Takata (1900–1980), a second-generation Japanese woman born in Hawaii, who later introduced Reiki to the West. There, it blended with New Age philosophies, evolving into a non-conventional healing and personal growth method now practiced worldwide.

(+)

Omamori and Ofuda

Widely used in daily life, *omamori* and *ofuda* are talismans believed to bring protection and good fortune. *Omamori* are small, embroidered fabric pouches dedicated to *kami* (Shintō deities) or Buddhas, sold at temples and shrines. People often carry them in their bags or cars, and each one serves a specific purpose based on its color and the deity it represents. They can safeguard travelers, promote children's health, help students excel in school, bring luck in love or work, or ensure a safe childbirth. These talismans should never be opened, as doing so diminishes their power. They are traditionally effective for one year, after which they should be returned to the temple or shrine where they were purchased for proper disposal.

Ofuda, on the other hand, are wooden or paper talismans, primarily distributed by Shintō shrines (though we can also find them in some Buddhist temples). They bear the name of a protective *kami* or the shrine itself, and are typically displayed in homes or specific locations to ward off misfortune — such as fires — and attract good fortune. One of the most well-known *ofuda* is the *jingū-taima*, a rice paper talisman distributed at the Ise Grand Shrine.

(+)

Chinkon

hinkon are pacification rituals designed to calm restless spirits and restore balance to the soul. The term itself literally means "calming the soul" and reflects the deep concern for vengeful and unsettled spirits known as *goryō*. These rituals were traditionally performed in cases of misfortune or illness when the influence of a resentful entity was suspected.

The form of *chinkon* varies across historical periods and traditions, but they are typically conducted by Shintō priests, who may invoke the assistance of various *kami* belonging to their pantheon. The ultimate goal is to pacify the aggrieved spirit or elevate it to the status of a guardian deity.

One notable variation is the institutional *chinkon-sai*, a state ritual codified as early as the seventh century. Its purpose was to purify and strengthen the emperor's spirit before he performed other important official ceremonies. Since the Meiji period, this ritual has been conducted within the Imperial Palace.

(+)

Misogiharai

arai and *misogi* are essential purification rituals in the Shintō tradition. *Harai* aims to remove *kegare* (impurity) and *tsumi* (sins or misfortune). The ceremony may involve symbolic purification with water or the use of an *ōnusa* (also called *haraegushi*), a wooden wand adorned with paper streamers, which is waved over the person or object being purified.

Misogi is a purification ritual performed under running water — whether by standing beneath a waterfall, immersing in a river, or pouring sacred water over oneself. It serves to cleanse impurities and is often the preliminary step in more complex rites, such as initiation ceremonies or the invocation of *kami*, which require a purified environment free of *kegare*.

The origins of *misogiharai* can be traced back to the *Kojiki* (*Records of Ancient Matters, 712*). While these practices are often part of broader rituals, some stand-alone ceremonies exist, such as the Ōharae Shiki, the Great Purification, which is performed at shrines every June 30 and December 31.

(+)

Jōrei and Okiyome

*J*ōrei and *okiyome* are purification practices found in certain New Religions, a term encompassing a range of syncretic, millenarian movements that emerged in the late 19th century, often centered around a charismatic, shamanic leader. Specifically, *jōrei* is associated with Sekai Kyūseikyō and Shinji Shūmeikai, while *okiyome* is practiced within the Mahikari sect.

Though variations exist among different traditions, the general structure involves the believer expressing gratitude to the founder of the faith, reciting specific prayers, and affirming a commitment to avoiding sources of impurity. An experienced practitioner then guides the believer toward healing through the laying on of hands over key energy points believed to accumulate impurities.

New Religions place significant emphasis on these healing rituals, which often become a central reason for followers' devotion and serve as a tangible demonstration of divine benevolence.

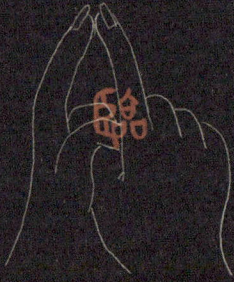

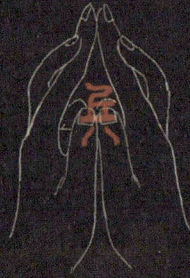

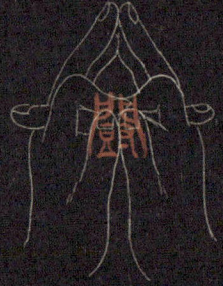

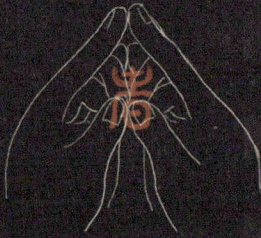

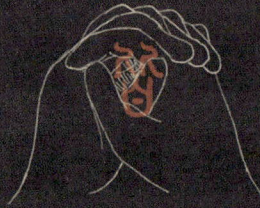

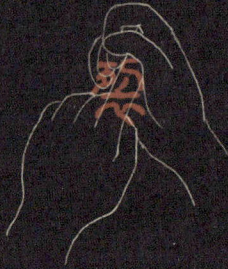

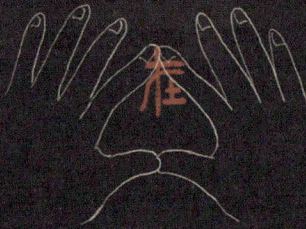

(+)

Kuji kiri

The term *kuji goshinpō* ("nine-character defensive technique") or, more commonly, *kuji kiri* ("nine characters and nine cuts") refers to a ritual involving nine symbolic hand signs (*mudra*), accompanied by a mantra consisting of nine syllables (*rin - pyo - to - sha - kai - jin - retsu - zai - zen*). Originally, these nine characters were inspired by a passage from the fourth-century Taoist text *Baopuzi* by Chinese philosopher Ge Hong, designed to ward off negative influences. The number nine holds great significance in Taoism, representing the "positive" aspect in the formation of hexagram lines in the *I Ching*.

This practice is commonly found in *shugendō*, Esoteric Buddhism, certain Shintō sects, and *onmyōdō* (the way of Yin and Yang). It serves as a protective ritual to dispel demonic influences. For instance, a sailor seeking protection from drowning might trace the nine cuts over the *kanji* for "sea" or "water."

Additionally, *kuji kiri* was adopted by the warrior class to boost focus and courage before battle, in time becoming a distinctive element of *ninja* traditions.

(+)

Kaji kitō

*K*aji kitō, meaning "spells and prayers," is a practice rooted in Nichiren Buddhism, a school that developed in Japan in the 13ᵗʰ century. The term *kaji* refers to the connection between humans and the divine, encapsulated in the phrase *sokushin jobutsu* ("becoming a Buddha in this very body"). *Kitō*, more specifically, denotes prayer, implying a transmission of power from a higher entity to a person or object.

The purpose of *kaji kitō* is to restore individual well-being by promoting healing, protection, and communion with the divine. A key figure in this practice is Kishimojin, the guardian deity of children, symbolizing transformation and compassion.

Various forms of *kaji kitō* have evolved over time, incorporating elements from other Buddhist traditions. Some practitioners use a *juzu* (a Buddhist rosary) to conjure up deities, while others employ a *bokken* (a wooden sword) as a tool for spiritual protection against evil forces.

(+)

Setsubun

Setsubun marks the day before the beginning of spring according to the lunar calendar. It typically falls in early February and symbolizes the end of winter and a ritual purification from negative forces. The festival traces its origins to Chinese traditions and was introduced to Japan in the eighth century. According to the *Shoku Nihongi* — a historical chronicle compiled during the Nara period — the earliest records of Setsubun date back to 706.

The modern form of the festival emerged during the Muromachi period (1336–1573), when noble and samurai households adopted the custom of throwing beans over their home's threshold. During the Edō period, this practice spread to the general population, evolving into the ritual we see today, which often involves a Buddhist monk or Shintō priest.

The most well-known custom sees people throwing beans outside their homes while chanting, *Oni wa soto! Fuku wa uchi!* ("Demons out! Fortune in!"). Public celebrations often feature individuals dressed as *oni* (demons), who are driven away by the crowd.

(+)

DIVINATION

(+)

Japanese divination arts boast a long, fascinating history rooted in the country's diverse religious and spiritual panorama. Japan has sought guidance from *kami* and spirits for support as to future events since the time of legendary Queen Himiko, and many of these practices formed an integral part of state rituals for years. As always, a host of folk traditions developed alongside the more institutional dimension, from *ninso uranai* to the Chinese zodiac, which entered the people's daily life through the centuries. A multifaceted universe shaped by a host of figures – from *miko* to *minkan fusha* – who, over time, sought supernatural insights into people's destinies. Today, divination practices are still a constant in daily life. Some examples: *omikuji*, the paper slips drawn at temples and shrines, or the belief in *yakudoshi*, the calamitous years of our lives. Still steeped in its age-old allure, these practices evoke the powerful and magical atmospheres of ancient Japan.

(+)

Miko

iko are priestesses in Shintō tradition, with origins believed to date back to the Jōmon (ca. 10,000–300 BC). Literally translated as "woman shaman" and commonly known as "shrine maidens," *miko* played a key role in ancient Shintō practice. They were believed to communicate with spirits through dreams and performed possession rituals to interact with the *kami*. These often took the form of magical-religious dances called *mikomai* or *mikokagura*, in which rhythmic movements led the maidens into trances.

Though *miko* once held great social and political influence, their role gradually diminished with the rise of Buddhism and the prohibition of certain Nara-period practices. Today, their duties have been stripped of nearly all religious or magical elements. However, the *miko*'s allure lives on in manga and anime, where they are often depicted with supernatural abilities – examples include Bishojo Senshi Sailor Moon, Your Name, and Inuyasha.

(+)

Minkan Fusha

The term *minkan fusha* refers to a wide range of folk religious practitioners who still operate across the Japanese archipelago. These female spiritual figures, whose roles span both Shintō and Buddhist traditions, are known by different names depending on the region and their practices.

Among the most well-known are women referred to as *kamisama* — individuals who, after experiencing illness or personal misfortune, embark on a spiritual journey and become mediators for *kami* or Buddhas, offering healing and protective rituals to those who seek their aid. Another notable group is the *itako* of the Tōhoku region — blind mediums who, following a rigorous apprenticeship in the mountains, are believed to possess the ability to summon the spirits of the dead, allowing communication with loved ones. Similarly, *yuta*, shamanic figures from Okinawa, serve as intermediaries between the human and spiritual realms.

These and other *minkan fusha* experienced a resurgence in popularity during Japan's postwar occultism boom, reinforcing their role in a society where folk spirituality persisted alongside rapid modernization.

(+)

Yakudoshi

In Japanese culture, there remains a widespread belief in *yakudoshi* — certain years in a person's life that are considered particularly unlucky. Likely of Chinese origin, with influences from *onmyōdō* (the traditional Japanese esoteric cosmology), the concept of *yakudoshi* designates different inauspicious ages for men and women. Women are believed to be at risk at ages 19, 33, and 37, while men should be cautious at 25, 42, and 61 — though variations exist depending on historical periods and geographical regions.

The calculation of *yakudoshi* follows the traditional Japanese method of age reckoning, where a person is considered one year old at birth. During these ill-fated years, it is advisable to avoid major life changes such as buying a house, changing jobs, getting married, or having children.

This form of superstition remains deeply ingrained in Japanese society. Every year, purification ceremonies known as *yakubarai* are held across the country to protect those entering a *yakudoshi* year from misfortune and evil spirits.

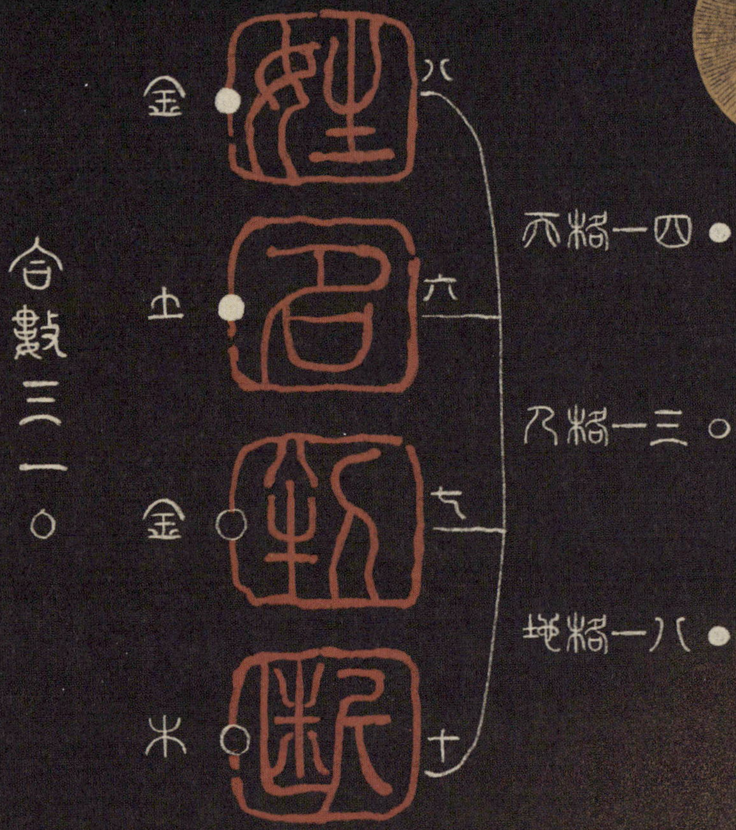

合數　三一〇

金　八

天排一四

土　六

尺排一三〇

金　七

地排一八

木　十

(+)

Seimei Handan

*S*eimei handan is an ancient form of onomancy – a name-based divination practice – that was introduced to Japan from China. It gained particular prominence during the Meiji period, when a nationwide registration system requiring both first and last names was implemented.

This complex divination method considers multiple factors but is primarily based on the number of strokes in the *kanji* characters of a person's name. Depending on the technique and the diviner, calculations may involve the stroke count of individual *kanji* or specific combinations of character elements. Certain numbers are deemed auspicious, while others are considered unlucky.

The Japanese often consult *seimei handan* when choosing names for their children or when artists select a stage name.

(+)

Amagoi

magoi are rain-invoking rituals rooted in ancient Shintō beliefs, which hold that *kami* have the power to control natural phenomena, including the weather.

Although practices vary by region, *amagoi* rituals share common elements such as lighting fires on mountaintops, invoking *kami* and Buddhas through ceremonies, and making pilgrimages to shrines. Traditionally, these rituals were performed by Shintō priests or *shugenja* (practitioners of *shugendō*, a syncretic ascetic tradition) and often involved dances, chants, and incantations, sometimes accompanied by sacred water to symbolize rainfall.

In ancient Japan, even emperors took part in *amagoi*. The *Nihon Shoki* chronicles an instance where Empress Kōgyoku performed a rain ritual that was followed by a powerful storm. Buddhism also contributed to this tradition, particularly within the Shingon school, which incorporated the recitation of specific *sutra* for rain.

Today, one of the most famous *amagoi* rituals takes place in Tsurugashima, Saitama Prefecture.

(+)

Feng Shui (Chinese Geomancy)

Feng shui, also known as Chinese geomancy, is a practice that dates all the way back to the Yangshao culture (5000–3000 BC) and has deep ties to ancient Chinese astronomy. It is an intricate philosophy that employs the concepts of Yin and Yang with the aim of harmonizing the environment with the life energy known as *qi*, thereby fostering well-being and prosperity.

Known in Japanese as *fūsui*, this practice was introduced to the Japanese archipelago in the seventh century and gradually came to influence various aspects of daily life and architecture. From home arrangement to interior design, the construction of sacred buildings, garden planning, and even the choice of colors and materials, Feng Shui provides auspicious solutions to encourage the flow of positive energy.

Today, this practice has spread far beyond Asia and continues to be used as a means of enhancing well-being and creating a balanced environment.

(+)

Jūnishi

The *jūnishi*, or Chinese zodiac, is a tradition that originated in China around the 11th century BC. It is based on the lunar calendar, a 12-year cycle, and a broader sexagenary cycle, which is still widely used in East Asia today.

Introduced to Japan in ancient times, the *jūnishi* is structured around 12 animals (rat, ox, tiger, rabbit, dragon, snake, horse, goat, monkey, rooster, dog, and boar), five elements (wood, earth, water, fire, and metal), and other foundational concepts of Chinese tradition.

This system is believed to influence individual personalities, events, and fortunes, based on the interaction between birth year, associated animal, and corresponding element. The *jūnishi* is tied to numerous legends explaining its origins and the sequence of animals. In addition to character analysis, it is also used to mark the hours of the day, make predictions about the future, and provide guidance on influencing one's yearly fate. For instance, 2025 is the Year of the Green Wood Snake, a symbol of wisdom, transformation, and peace.

A

B

O

AB

(+)

Ketsueki-gata

I n Japanese culture, there is still a widespread belief that a person's blood type (*ketsueki-gata*) can serve as a marker of their personality, tendencies, and even their relationship and romantic preferences.

Each of the four blood types is associated with specific traits: type A individuals are viewed as responsible and organized but also reserved; type B people are thought to be creative and passionate but also self-centered; type AB is seen as a combination of both A and B, characterized by traits of unpredictability; type O individuals are believed to be charismatic but also egocentric.

These beliefs trace back to the publications of Masahiko Nomi in the 1970s, and although the scientific community has largely discredited them, his works still enjoy widespread popularity in popular culture. Blood type is often discussed in various social settings, including dating websites, where it is sometimes used to predict the success of a romantic meeting.

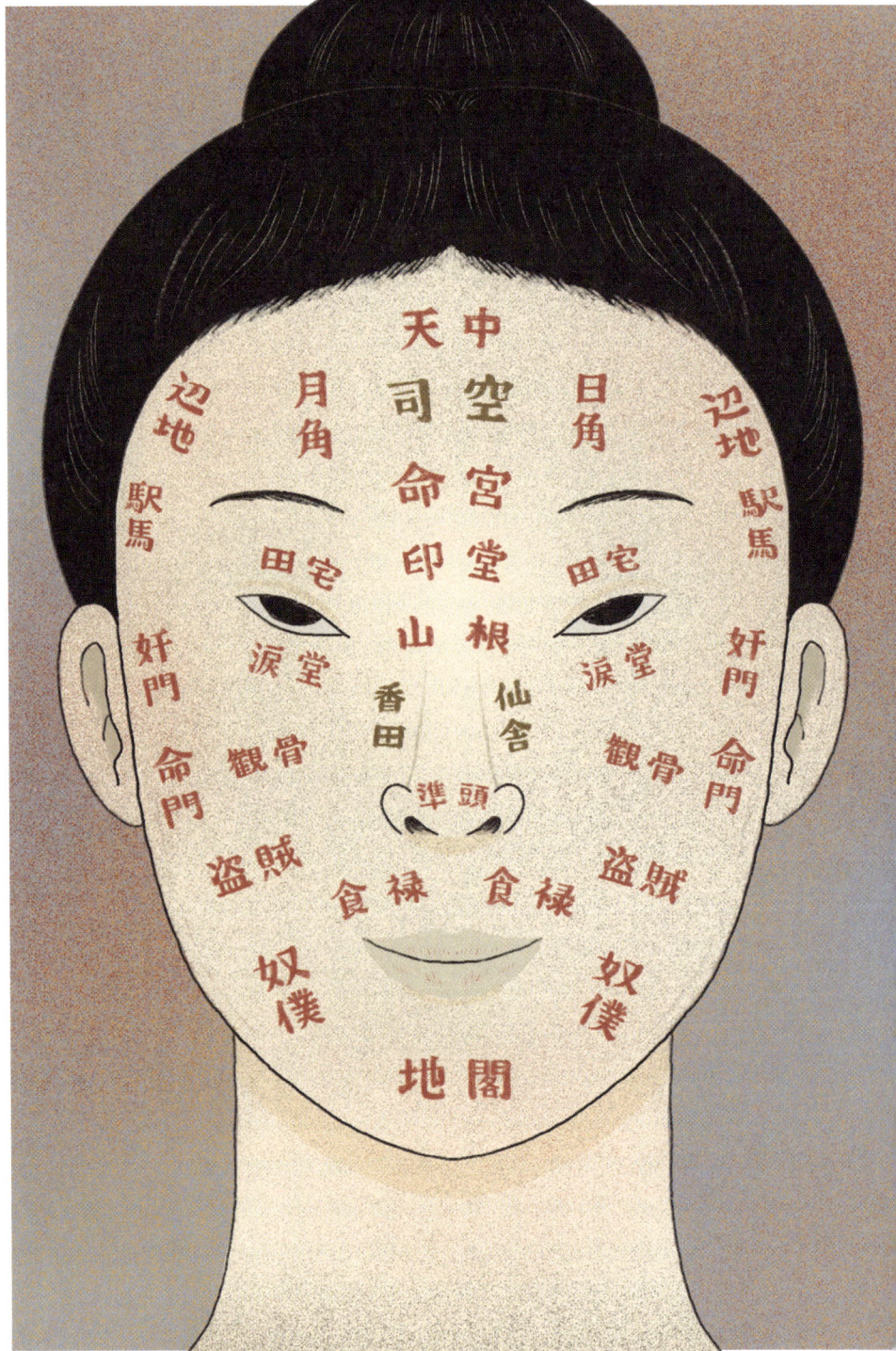

⟨✦⟩

Ninsō Uranai

Known in Japan as *ninsō uranai*, physiognomy is an ancient practice that involves interpreting the features of a person's face to deduce their personality traits and make predictions about their future fortunes. For instance, according to this tradition, a wide nose may indicate a generous person, while almond-shaped eyes might suggest a shrewd nature.

Like many traditional practices, physiognomy has its roots in Chinese culture, with many references to numerology, and was introduced to Japan during the Heian period. It eventually integrated with Shintō and Buddhist beliefs. During the Genroku period (1688–1704), it became more widespread among the population due to the introduction of various texts from the mainland. It was during this time that physiognomy began to be used to sketch the personalities of characters in *ukiyo-e* prints and other works.

Today, its popularity is more limited, with face readings typically being performed at social events or as a form of entertainment.

(✛)

Omikuji

The term *omikuji* (literally "lottery") refers to small paper slips that worshippers receive at Shintō shrines and Buddhist temples, typically in exchange for a donation. These slips contain fortunes and advice about the future.

The practice dates back to the Heian period, particularly to the monk Ganzan Daishi, who formalized the *Ganzan Daishi Hyakusen*, a set of one hundred slips featuring various combinations of four five-character verses. *Omikuji* gained popularity during the Edō period and further diversified in the Meiji period: those found in temples often contained references to Classical Chinese, while those in shrines were inspired by Japanese poetry. The fortunes on *omikuji* fall into seven possible categories: *dai-kichi* (great fortune), *kichi* (fortune), *shō-kichi* (small fortune), *han-kichi* (half fortune), *sue-kichi* (future fortune), *sue-shō-kichi* (small future fortune), and *kyō* (misfortune).

If the *omikuji* predicts bad luck, it is customary to tie the slip to a designated tree at the shrine, a practice believed to ward off evil spirits.

明治六年来暑表

四方拝月旦
始　祭月旦
元始　祭月旦
孝明天皇祭正月三十日
春季皇霊祭三月廿一日
紀元節二月十一日
神武天皇　即位之年
神武天皇祭四月三日
神嘗祭九月十七日
天長節十一月三日
秋季皇霊祭九月廿三日
新嘗祭十一月廿三日

神武天皇

歳徳

令和七年神宮暦

明治二十七年ノ

歳徳　金神

(+)

Koyomi

The *koyomi* (almanac), a traditional tool for consultation and divination, remains a common feature of Japanese daily life. Originally introduced from China (possibly as early as the sixth century), the *koyomi* typically includes: *rokuyō*, a system classifying days as auspicious or inauspicious; lunar phases; and the old date according to the lunisolar calendar, which divided the year into twenty-four periods before Japan adopted the Gregorian calendar on January 1, 1873.

Depending on the region, some *koyomi* also feature information on tides and an extensive list of Shintō and Buddhist festivals.

During the Meiji period, the widespread publication of official almanacs (*honreki*) was led by the Ise Shrine and authorized printing houses across Japan. At the same time, unofficial almanacs known as *obakegoyomi* ("phantom almanacs") also became popular. These were published by unauthorized printers and contained alternative details or more localized information tailored to specific regions.

(+)

DEITIES

(+)

In Japan, the supernatural world is rich in nuance, inhabited by more or less benevolent figures who coexist with humans. On one hand we find *kami*, deities of the Shintō pantheon — foremost among them Amaterasu Ōmikami, the great Sun Goddess from whom the imperial family is said to descend. Alongside them exists a realm of figures and names drawn from ancient legends, interacting with the human world in various ways. Yet *kami* can also be local spirits, deeply tied to nature's hues, reminding us that all living beings carry a divine spark within. Japan is also home to a host of Buddhist deities, introduced from the continent with their own stories and traditions: from the *bodhisattva* (or "*bosatsu*" in Japanese) Jizō to the Seven Gods of Fortune, Buddhist traditions blend seamlessly and imaginatively with native beliefs, shaping a multifaceted and captivating spiritual dimension that still permeates contemporary tales.

(+)

Amaterasu

oddess of the Sun and mythological ancestress of the Imperial Dynasty, Amaterasu Ōmikami is the central *kami* in Shintō. According to the *Kojiki*, Amaterasu is the first-born daughter of Izanagi, the father of all the *kami* and the creator of the lands along with Izanami. The Sun Goddess was born from the god's left eye while he was purifying himself after his escape from the world of the dead. By his will, she became the ruler of Takamagahara, the High Celestial Plains where the *kami* reside.

One of the most famous mythical episodes is the eclipse: after a quarrel with her brother Susanō, Amaterasu shut herself in a cave, plunging the world into darkness. It was the goddess Ame no Uzume who lured her out of hiding and restored the light.

Amaterasu is also the grandmother of Ninigi no Mikoto, sent by the goddess to pacify Japan. To help him complete his mission, she bestowed upon him the three sacred regalia (see p. 19), which were passed down from Ninigi to his grandson, Jinmu, the first emperor of Japan.

(+)

Jizō

In Buddhist tradition, Jizō (Kṣitigarbha in India) is defined as a *bosatsu*, or *bodhisattva*, a unique figure who has attained Buddhahood but chooses to give up Nirvana so as to continue helping all living beings on their path to enlightenment.

There are other popular *bosatsu* (such as Amida or Kannon) in Japan, but Jizō in particular is considered the savior from the Buddhist hells: he is the one who can guide souls through the various levels of reincarnation and allow them to approach Nirvana.

Statues depicting Jizō are widespread throughout Japan, with the distinctive iconography of a child monk with a shaved head, often holding a pilgrim's staff and wearing a red bib. The staff reminds us that Jizō is also the protector of travelers. His figure is further associated with the imagery of *mizuko*, the souls of unborn or deceased infants, which gather on the banks of the Sanzu, the river of hell, waiting for Jizō to intervene and grant them rebirth.

(+)

Daruma

The *daruma* is a particular votive object, a small doll with no arms or legs representing Bodhidharma, the founder of Zen. There are many legends surrounding this monk, but the most widely known tells that he meditated for such a long time — nine years — that his arms and legs eventually atrophied and fell off.

It is also said that, during his meditation, the monk fell asleep at one point: upon waking, furious at his mistake, he decided to cut off his eyelids so he would never again risk succumbing to sleep.

The votive doll takes on the monk's altered appearance: its body is round and lacking limbs, and there are two white circles where its eyes should be. Tradition holds that one of the pupils should be drawn with black ink while making a wish: once the wish is granted, the second pupil can be drawn as well.

(+)

Ame no Uzume

Kami of the Dawn, it is thanks to her that the Sun returned to shine on the Earth after Amaterasu had retreated into a cave following an argument with her brother, as narrated in the *Kojiki*. The *kami* tried for a long time to get the ruler to come out of hiding, but their prayers were in vain.

That is when Ame no Uzume intervened: she tied a mirror to the branch of a nearby tree and began dancing with increasingly frantic movements, disrobing and causing the laughter of all the *kami*. Curious and amazed by the laughter, Amaterasu decided to move the stone in front of the cave to peek out. The motion was enough for her face to be reflected in the mirror hanging from Ame no Uzume's branch: the vision distracted the Sun Goddess, who was then drawn out of the cave.

Ame no Uzume is considered the patroness of sacred dances, including *bugaku*, and the ancestress of shamans: her dance is thought to be an ecstatic ritual to communicate with the *kami*.

(+)

The Seven Gods of Fortune

The Seven Gods of Fortune, or Shichifukujin, are a group of popular deities associated with happiness, longevity, and good fortune, who grant rewards to the faithful. They are Bishamonten, Daikokuten, Ebisu, Fukurokuju, Jurōjin, Hotei, and Benzaiten, the only one with distinctly feminine traits.

Their origins are diverse and include Taoist influences (Jurōjin), Hindu influences (Benzaiten), Buddhist influences (Bishamonten), and more localized influences (Ebisu). Initially, these deities were worshipped individually: Daikokuten, for example, was venerated as the protector of commerce, and Benzaiten was the patroness of the arts. They later appeared together in the 16th century, but their canonization dates back to the Tokugawa shogunate, when their appearance was also codified.

The Shichifukujin are among the most beloved figures in Japanese popular tradition and often appear in the visual arts, theater, and contemporary pop culture.

HISTORICAL FIGURES

Japanese history is rich in historical and semi-mythological figures whose extraordinary adventures often intertwine with the spiritual world. From the legendary Himiko – the first recorded queen of Japan – to Shōtoku Taishi and Yamato Takeru, countless rulers and emperors are said to have interacted with supernatural forces, harnessing divine power to secure victory in battle or defeat fearsome monsters. Though historical and archaeological evidence may not always confirm their existence, their deeds have been preserved in ancient texts and continue to shape Japan's cultural heritage and collective imagination. Even in modern and contemporary times, several prominent figures have been drawn to the supernatural world, living at its margins or engaging with it in meaningful ways. Representing both power and spirituality, these figures still influence Japanese culture today, often seen as symbols of a return to tradition in a world that is rapidly moving toward modernity.

(✦)

Himiko

Himiko (170?—248), the first female ruler of Japan, appears as far back as the *Book of Wei* (part of the Records of the Three Kingdoms), dating back to the third century. This text contains the earliest known reference to the island kingdom of Yamatai, which was ruled by a queen — Himiko — chosen by the people to end the prolonged warfare that had plagued the land.

Himiko is typically regarded as Japan's first shaman-queen, a figure capable of mediating between the human and divine realms. She was assisted by her brother, Akatsuki, and wielded magical-religious powers that enabled her to commune with the gods through prayers and possession rituals. Few individuals were allowed to approach her; among them, her most trusted confidant was her brother, who conveyed her divine oracles to the people.

This pattern recurs throughout ancient Japanese history: a reigning woman endowed with shamanic and divinatory powers, accompanied by a male — often her brother — who takes on an increasingly dominant role. Over time, this dynamic helped pave the way for a male-dominated imperial succession.

(+)

Jinmu

Jinmu (711–585 BC) is the legendary first emperor of Japan and the founder of the ruling dynasty. According to the *Kojiki* and *Nihonshoki*, he was the grandson of Ninigi no Mikoto, who had been sent by Amaterasu to rule over the earthly realm. He is also said to have taken a second wife, Himetataraisuzu-hime, a descendant of Susanō, and to have lived an extraordinarily long life, reaching the age of 126.

The beginning of his reign is traditionally dated to February 11, 660 BC, when, according to legend, Jinmu reached the central lands of Yamato and took command of the local tribes. Though historical sources disagree on this chronology, the story is believed to reflect an actual migration of western tribes who established control over the more eastern territories of the archipelago.

Jinmu was particularly venerated during the Meiji period, and to this day, February 11 is celebrated as Japan's Foundation Day.

(+)

Sugawara no Michizane

Sugawara no Michizane (845–903) is one of the most renowned figures in Japan's ancient history. Born into a noble family during the Heian period, he quickly excelled in his studies, becoming a poet and court scholar. From 886 onward, he served as governor of Sanuki Province (on Shikoku) and steadily rose in rank thanks to the trust of Emperor Uda.

Uda's son and successor, Emperor Daigo, appointed him *udaijin* (minister of the right), but in 901, the Fujiwara clan accused him of treason and persuaded the emperor to exile him to Kyushu, where he died in 903. Soon after, Japan was struck by a series of extraordinary calamities – storms, fires, and sudden deaths – leading the court to suspect they were caused by Michizane's vengeful spirit. To appease him, the emperor posthumously revoked the charges, restored his titles, and deified him as Tenjin, God of Thunder.

Still today, students pay homage to Sugawara no Michizane at Dazaifu Tenmangu Shrine near Fukuoka, seeking his blessing for academic success.

(+)

Jingū

Jingū (169?–269) is a semi-legendary empress, wife of Emperor Chūai (who reigned from 192 to 200) and regent for their son Ōjin. According to legend, with the aid of the sea god Ryūjin, she controlled the waters and led a conquest of Korea. The tale also claims that Ōjin – later deified as Hachiman, the God of War – remained in her womb for three years, allowing her to complete her campaign before returning to Japan to give birth.

This account lacks historical credibility, and while Japan did exert some influence over the Korean Peninsula in the fourth century, Jingū's exploits are largely fictional. Her very existence is difficult to verify, but she appears to fit within the context of a matriarchal society that existed in western Japan, as suggested by Chinese records and the figure of Himiko.

The two women share many similarities, and Jingū herself is depicted as a powerful shaman and fearless warrior, armed with a sword and bow.

(✦)

Ōjin

Ōjin (third to fourth century) is a semi-legendary emperor and one of the most important figures in Shintō mythology and the texts of the *Kojiki* and *Nihonshoki*. Born to Empress Jingū (according to legend, after a three-year gestation) and Emperor Chūai, Ōjin is renowned for consolidating imperial power, supporting land reforms, and promoting cultural exchanges with China and the Korean Peninsula.

It is said that Confucianism was introduced during his reign, while highly elaborate spinning techniques spread from Korea.

Upon his death, Ōjin was deified as Hachiman, also known as Yahata no Kami, the *kami* of eight banners. Popular in both Buddhism and *shugendō*, Hachiman, as the *kami* of war, was a central figure for the Kamakura shogunate (1185–1333), and his legacy endures to this day. Thousands of shrines are dedicated to him, making him one of the most widely venerated deities alongside Inari and Tenjin.

(+)

Shōtoku Taishi

Shōtoku Taishi (574–622), also known as Umayado, was the son of Emperor Yōmei and served as prince regent to his aunt, Empress Suiko, from 593. He is one of the most significant figures of ancient Japan, credited with spreading Buddhism throughout the archipelago with the support of the Soga clan after their victory over the Mononobe, who had upheld Shintō.

A scholar of continental affairs, he sent the first official embassy to China in 607, initiating the centralization of power in imperial hands and an in-depth governmental reorganization inspired by a Chinese-style meritocracy.

Shōtoku Taishi is also attributed with the famous *Seventeen-Article Constitution*, a code outlining ethical and moral principles for the ruling class. According to tradition, he founded Hōryūji, a magnificent Buddhist complex in Nara, whose pagoda is the oldest surviving wooden structure in the world.

(+)

Yamato Takeru

Yamato Takeru (72?–114), , also known as Prince Ousu, is a semi-legendary figure of the first century whose deeds are primarily recounted in the *Kojiki* and *Nihonshoki*. His name means "the warrior of Yamato," and he is regarded as one of the founders of the nation, as well as the quintessential tragic hero of Japanese tradition.

According to legend, Yamato Takeru accidentally killed his brother, provoking the anger of his father, Emperor Keikō, who sent him to Kyūshū to subdue the rebellious Kumaso tribes. There, Yamato Takeru triumphed through cunning, disguising himself as a woman. He was later dispatched to eastern Japan to bring other peoples under Yamato rule.

A key aspect of his story is his connection to the Ise Grand Shrine, founded by his aunt, who bestowed upon him the sword Kusanagi, one of the three imperial regalia. With this weapon, the hero was able to vanquish his enemies and bring peace to the land. Various accounts exist of his death, but according to legend, he fell in Nobono, in present-day Mie Prefecture, in a duel fought without the sword Kusanagi.

(+)

Abe no Seimei

A be no Seimei (921–1005) was one of the most power-ful *onmyōji* – masters of *onmyōdō* – at the Heian court. Over the years, he became so famous that by the late 10th century, the Ministry of *Onmyōdō* was under the control of the Abe family.

His popularity gave rise to numerous legends, many of which were collected in the *Konjaku Monogatari* ("Anthology of Tales from the Past and Present") in the 12th century. According to these accounts, Seimei was not entirely human, and his mother was said to be Kuzunoha, a powerful *kitsune*.

He had various duties at the Heian court, including analyzing unusual events, performing exorcisms, and practicing geoman-cy. His personal seal was the *seiman*, a five-pointed star resem-bling a pentagram, associated with the five Chinese elements. After his death, this symbol became one of the main emblems of *onmyōdō*. His renown is also linked to his numerous battles against *oni* (see p. 125), including Shutendōji, whose hiding place Seimei is said to have discovered.

(+)

Takashima Kaemon

Takashima Kaemon (1832–1914) was an entrepreneur active between the 19th and 20th centuries, now recognized as one of the key figures in modern divination. A passionate student of the *I Ching*, the Chinese *Book of Changes*, Takashima extensively studied the interpretations of its 64 hexagrams. He even used predictions derived from the text for financial investments, which proved successful before the great earthquake of 1854.

His fortunes did not last long, however — after accumulating heavy debts, he was convicted and imprisoned for seven years. During his time in prison, he continued studying the *I Ching* and, upon his release, published his ten-volume work *Takashima Ekidan* in 1886, on interpreting the Chinese classics. The book was a success, was translated into Chinese, and brought him into contact with influential figures such as Itō Hirobumi. He eventually began using the *I Ching* to make predictions for public and military affairs.

The popularity of *Takashima Ekidan* led to the publication of numerous other works inspired by his studies, blending his reputation with hexagram analysis and other practices such as physiognomy and palm reading.

(+)

Fujita Kototome

Fujita Kototome, also known as Fujita Kotohime (1938–1994), was a highly popular fortune teller and psychic in the postwar era. Born in Fukuoka, Kyūshū, her childhood was marked by war and her parents' divorce. It is said that at the age of 9, she was possessed by the spirit of a fox, and by 11, newspapers were already writing about her.

During the 1950s and 1960s, her reputation as a psychic fortune teller grew, making her a familiar face in newspapers and on television. Her success was largely due to the influential connections she built over the years, including ties to the world of politics — even with Prime Minister Kishi — and business.

In the late 1960s, she became embroiled in legal troubles following a fire for which she was found responsible. The ensuing scandal led to a swift decline in her fame, and she relocated to Hawaii in 1973. She met a tragic end in 1994 when she was shot and killed in Honolulu along with her son, Goro. The court convicted Raita Fukusaku, an acquaintance of Goro's, for the murders; Fukusaku later died in prison under mysterious circumstances in 2024.

(+)

Kurihara Sumiko

K urihara Sumiko (1930–2019) was a renowned fortune teller, active since the 1950s. After a difficult childhood, several family misfortunes — including the loss of a daughter — and an apprenticeship as a fortune teller, she began practicing near the Isetan department store in Shinjuku; in fact, the media soon dubbed her "the Mother of Shinjuku."

Her practice combined astrology, palm reading, and onomancy (*seimei handan*). Famous in Tokyo's most prominent districts, she worked for over 50 years, conducting more than three million consultations, publishing numerous books, and making frequent public appearances.

In 2006, to mark her fifty years in the profession, the TV film *Shinjuku no haha monogatari* ("The Story of the Mother of Shinjuku") was broadcast, featuring interviews with Kurihara herself and her son, Tatsuya. After her passing, her practice was taken over by Tatsuya, who continues her work in the Shinjuku area.

(+)

CREATURES

(+)

Yōkai are supernatural creatures that define Japanese folklore, more popular today than ever thanks to a renewed fascination — both in Japan and globally — with the mysterious and sometimes terrifying world of monsters and spirits. *Yōkai* are ambivalent beings: fearsome yet curious and sociable. Their interactions with humans can bring about great misfortune or extraordinary luck. Alongside the ever-popular *kitsune*, the iconic fox messenger of the gods, legends feature other striking figures such as the *tengu*, a masterful warrior with unparalleled powers, and the *yuki-onna*, a chilling presence that threatens to bring ruin to hapless souls who encounter her on winter days. As quintessential protagonists of folktales, these creatures provide a lens through which to explore the complexities of collective dynamics and the injustices that often shaped society. They also remind us, once again, of the immense syncretic and creative power of Japan's spiritual traditions, weaving captivating narratives that transcend the boundaries of individual faiths.

(+)

Yamauba

*Y*amauba (or *yamanba*) are mountain-dwelling *yōkai* who resemble old women. Their iconography is especially picturesque: a thin body wrapped in an old, threadbare kimono, long white hair to ensnare their pray, an enormous mouth, and a chilling gaze.

Endowed with great magical powers, they can control the forces of nature and are often shapeshifters, turning into young women so as to lure and then devour travelers. In some cases, however, *yamauba* are benevolent figures: a key example is the legend of Kintarō, the "golden boy" abandoned by his mother in the mountains and raised by a *yamauba*, who grants him extraordinary powers and the ability to become an invincible warrior.

Frequently depicted in manga and literature, *yamauba* might have ties to the tradition of *ubasute*, in which elderly people were abandoned in the mountains as a form of population control.

(+)

Kitsune

The *kitsune* is the Japanese shapeshifting fox, a benevolent messenger or a cunning trickster, known for its ambiguous nature. Since it feeds on mice and rats — both harmful to crops — it is regarded as a protector of rice fields. Because of this benevolent aspect, it is often depicted as a servant of Inari, the *kami* of rice cultivation and commerce, and statues of *kitsune* can be found in many shrines.

However, the *kitsune* is also a powerful trickster capable of taking on a female form to deceive humans. This interpretation may stem from the fox's habit of preying on farm animals, or perhaps from its association with the jackal in Indian and Buddhist traditions, where the animal is considered malevolent.

In general, *kitsune* are believed to live for hundreds or even thousands of years, gaining greater powers as they age and developing a complex hierarchy. The most powerful ones grow up to nine tails and eventually become celestial foxes, who grant wishes to devoted believers.

(+)

Kappa

Ambiguous and often dangerous *yōkai*, *kappa* are water spirits that inhabit rivers, lakes, and ponds. Their appearance is unmistakable: their bodies resemble those of children or monkeys, but they are bluish-green, covered in scales or a turtle-like shell. Atop their heads is a "dish" filled with water — if it spills or breaks, they lose all their powers.

Traditionally, *kappa* were feared creatures, known for dragging unsuspecting swimmers underwater by their feet. However, some legends depict them as benevolent beings, willing to offer favors to humans. The famous *kappamaki* sushi roll owes its name to the *kappa*'s love of cucumbers and the resemblance between the sliced vegetable and the dish on their heads.

Some stories tell of humans tricking *kappa* into granting favors: obsessed with politeness, they are compelled to bow in return when greeted. This act causes the water in their dish to spill, instantly robbing them of their powers.

(+)

Tanuki

Tanuki are *yōkai* inspired by the *Nyctereutes procyonoides*, a canid native to East Asia. These spirits, with a cheerful nature, appear as early as the Nara period. Known as powerful tricksters, they inhabit forests and villages, possessing the ability to transform into any object or living being. In folklore, they are often depicted with prominent bellies, which they playfully drum on to scare travelers or hunters they meet.

Over time, the legends have focused particularly on their playful nature, and *tanuki* are often regarded as spirits of good fortune. They are also symbols of fun and drunkenness: in many stories, they transform into humans to join the villagers and indulge in revelry by drinking to excess.

In their real-world form, *tanuki* are still found in several parts of Japan and are frequently sighted near urban centers, where they approach in search of food.

(+)

Tengu

*T*engu are powerful spirits of the mountains and forests, appearing as far back as the ancient texts of the *Nihonshoki* and *Konjaku Monogatari*. Linked to Chinese traditions, their name means "heavenly dogs," and they are generally depicted with a red face, long nose, and bird-like features, such as a beak or wings. They can also fly.

In Buddhism, they appear as terrible warrior demons, but over time they evolved into more ambiguous figures — beings that could instill fear in humans while also offering protection. They are also associated with *shugendō*, often depicted wearing the robes of the *yamabushi*, the ascetic monks of the mountains.

It is said that *tengu*, experts in martial arts, abduct children who become lost in the mountains, training them in combat and allowing them to return to the human world with supernatural powers. Minamoto no Yoshitsune, a great 12th-century warrior, is said to have been trained by these powerful beings, gaining his great military skills from them.

(+)

Bakeneko

akeneko are supernatural cats with great magical powers and shapeshifting *yōkai*. They are found throughout Japan — also in the version known as *nekomata*, characterized by a forked tail. These creatures can dance, take on human forms, speak to people, cast curses, and even animate the dead. Their magical abilities manifest when the animal reaches an advanced age: just like foxes, the older they get, the more powerful they become.

As with many traditional *yōkai*, *bakeneko* are ambiguous figures: many legends tell of feline spirits seeking revenge for mistreatment suffered during their lives, often going so far as to devour their wrongdoers and replace them to exact their revenge. In other stories, however, *bakeneko* are closely linked with certain human families: they protect them from evil, bring them good fortune, and may even steal their owners' bodies to keep them with them.

The fame of the *bakeneko* has remained strong since the Edō period, and they continue to be among the most beloved subjects in popular culture.

(+)

Yuki-onna

*Y*uki-onna (Snow Woman) is a *yōkai* that takes the form of a beautiful young woman dressed in a white kimono, a color traditionally associated with death in Japanese culture. Her pale skin and chilling gaze add to her eerie presence.

Although she may appear calm and serene, she is ruthless toward the humans (often men) who encounter her. She has the power to freeze them instantly with her breath, drain their vital energy, or lead them astray, ultimately causing them to die in the snow. In some versions of the legend, the *Yuki-onna* is seen holding a child, and when the unfortunate traveler attempts to take the child, he is frozen to death.

The origins of this figure seem to trace back to the Muromachi period, particularly in the Tōhoku region, where snow represents a tangible threat. Up until the 18th century, this *yōkai* was generally depicted as an unforgiving and merciless being. Over time, however, the legends evolved to include variations where the *Yuki-onna* falls in love with a human and marries him, until the relationship takes a tragic turn when the man breaks a promise.

(+)

Oni

*O*ni are giant demonic figures, possessing supernatural strength and a terrifying appearance. They often have blue or red skin, horns on their heads, three-fingered hands, clawed feet, and sometimes even three flaming eyes.

They dwell in mountain caves and can change shape to deceive humans and lay waste to their villages. Their origins trace back to China, with strong Hindu and Buddhist influences, and legends link them to the goddess Izanami.

In folklore, *oni* are often man-eaters, capable of devouring a person in a single bite (*onihitokuchi*). Their cruelty is believed to symbolize the violence of wars and natural disasters that plagued ancient Japan. Written records mention *oni* as early as the eighth century, in the *Kojiki* and *Nihonshoki*, yet these demonic beings remain ever-present in Japanese culture. Beyond their role in purification rituals during festivals like Setsubun, *oni* continue to inspire popular culture, appearing in works such as the iconic manga *Demon Slayer* and *Urusei Yatsura* (featuring the famous character Lum).

Marianna Zanetta

(+)

Marianna Zanetta has a Ph.D. in religions and thought systems (Université Sorbonne) and in cultural anthropology (Università degli Studi di Torino). Since 2012, she has conducted field research in Japan on folk and shamanic religious practices, funeral rites, and the role of women in society and contemporary religions. Since 2017, she has served as the president of the Inari Association for the promotion of Japanese culture in Italy and has worked with various organizations to organize events and meetings. She has been teaching Sociology of Cultural Processes at the Scuola di Psicologia Clinica at the Università degli Studi di Torino since 2021.

Asuka Ozumi

(+)

Following a Ph.D. in South and East Asian studies at the Università degli Studi di Napoli l'Orientale, Asuka Ozumi held Japanese language and translation classes for several institutes. She's been president of the CeSAO (Center for Eastern Asian Studies) cultural association since 2016. She also works with several publishing companies as a consultant and translator of manga, fiction, and nonfiction. She's currently a teacher at the Università di Torino, where she teaches Japanese.

Danilo Kato

(+)

Danilo Kato is an artist and illustrator from São Paulo. He embarked on a career as a graphic designer following a degree in industrial design. After collaborating with prestigious agencies, including MTV, he continued to pursue his passions as a freelancer. Born in Brazil and raised in Japan, Kato reveals the influences of both cultures in his art. His intricate works invite viewers to reflect upon their feelings through themes such as love, death, nature, and spirituality.